THE **7** CONTINENTS

SOUTH AMERICA

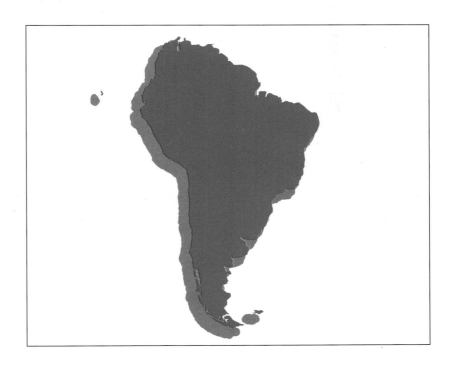

APRIL PULLEY SAYRE

TWENTY-FIRST CENTURY BOOKS
BROOKFIELD, CONNECTICUT

For my mother, who crash landed in the Amazon and was mistaken for Grace Kelly.

—A.P.S.

Published by Twenty-First Century Books
A Division of The Millbrook Press, Inc.
2 Old New Milford Road
Brookfield, Connecticut 06804

Text copyright © 1999 by April Pulley Sayre
Maps by Joe LeMonnier
All rights reserved.

Library of Congress Cataloging-in-Publication Data
Sayre, April Pulley.
South America / April Pulley Sayre
p. cm.—(The seven continents)
Includes bibliographical references and index.
Summary: Describes the geography, weather and climate, and plants and animals of
South America, a continent of contrasts.
ISBN 0-7613-1366-4 (lib. bdg.)
1. South America—Geography—Juvenile literature. 2. Natural
history—South America—Juvenile literature. 3. South America—Juvenile literature.
[1. South America.] I. Title. II. Series: Sayre, April Pulley. 7 continents.
F2208.5.S29 1999
918—dc21   98-30688
                                            CIP
                                            AC

Printed in the United States of America
5 4 3 2 1

Photo Credits

Cover photograph courtesy of Peter Arnold, Inc. (© Arnold Newman)

Photographs courtesy of SuperStock: pp. 8 (© J. Warden), 14 (© T. Linck), 38 (© Herbert Lanks); Tom Stack & Associates: pp. 12 (© Manfred Gottschalk), 46 (© Inga Spence); IDRC: p. 19; © Michael O. Dillon: p. 21; Photo Researchers: pp. 25 (© Jeff Greenberg), 26 (© C. Whiddington), 34 (© F. Gohier), 42 (© M. Philip Kahl), 52 (© Gregory G. Dimijian), 54 (© Asa C. Thoresen), 56 (© Leonide Principe); SABA: p. 22 (© Shepard Sherbell); Peter Arnold, Inc.: pp. 10 (© Luiz C. Marigo), 32 (© Martha Cooper), 40 (© Shafer & Hill), 43 (© Steve Kaufman), 45 (© Roland Seitre), 50 (© Luiz C. Marigo).

CONTENTS

INTRODUCTION

CONTINENTS: WHERE WE STAND

The ground you stand on may seem solid and stable, but it's really moving all the time. How is that possible? Because all of the earth's continents, islands, oceans, and people ride on tectonic plates. These plates, which are huge slabs of the earth's crust, float on top of hot, melted rock below. One plate may carry a whole continent and a piece of an ocean. Another may carry only a few islands and some ocean. The plates shift, slide, and even bump together slowly as the molten rock below them flows.

Plate edges are where the action is, geologically speaking. That's where volcanoes erupt and earthquakes shake the land. Tectonic plates collide, gradually crumpling continents into folds that become mountains. Dry land, or ocean floor, can be made at these plate edges. Melted rock, spurting out of volcanoes or oozing out of cracks between plates, cools and solidifies. Dry land, or ocean floor, can also be destroyed here, as the edge of one tectonic plate slips underneath another. The moving, grinding plates create tremendous pressure and heat, which melts the rock, turning it into semisolid material.

Continents, the world's largest landmasses, the rock rafts where we live, ride on this shifting puzzle of tectonic plates. These continents are made of material that floated to the surface when much of the earth was hot and liquid long ago. The floating material then cooled and became solid. Two hundred and fifty million years ago there was only one continent, the supercontinent Pangaea, surrounded by one ocean, Panthalassa. But since then, the tectonic plates have moved, breaking apart the continents and rearranging them. Today there are seven continents: North America, South America, Europe, Asia, Africa, Australia, and Antarctica.

250 Million Years Ago

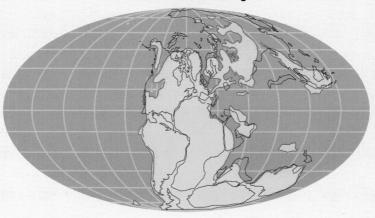

Two hundred and fifty million years ago there was only one continent and one ocean, as shown above. (Rough shapes the continents would eventually take are outlined in black.) The view below shows where the seven continents are today. These positions will continue to change slowly as tectonic plates shift.

Present Day

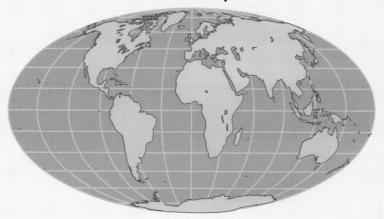

Each continent has its own unique character and conditions, shaped by its history and position on the earth. Europe, which is connected to Asia, has lots of coastline and moist, ocean air. Australia, meanwhile, is influenced by its neighbor, Antarctica, which sends cool currents northward to its shores. North America and South America were once separated, but are now connected by Panama. Over the years, animals, from ancient camels to armadillos, have traveled the bridge in between these two continents.

A continent's landscape, geology, weather, and natural communities affect almost every human action taken on that continent, from planting a seed to waging a war. Rivers become the borders of countries. Soil determines what we can grow. Weather and climate affect our cultures—what we feel, how we dress, even how we celebrate.

Understanding continents can give us a deeper knowledge of the earth—its plants, animals, and people. It can help us see behind news headlines to appreciate the forces that shape world events. Such knowledge can be helpful, especially in a world that's constantly changing and shifting, down to the very earth beneath our feet.

This dramatic formation is found where the Andes Mountains run through Chile.

ONE

KEYS TO THE
CONTINENT

When people think of South America, many think first of the Amazon—the tremendous river and the vast rain forest that surrounds it. Incredibly big, the Amazon River carries one fifth of the world's fresh water—more water than any other river on earth. It also drains 1,000 rivers and supports more than 1,300 species of fish—more fish species than the entire Atlantic Ocean!

The Amazon region, also called Amazonia, is home to monkeys and macaws, army ants and anteaters, pit vipers, puffbirds, and piranhas. Its species diversity—variety of animal and plant types—is unmatched anywhere else on earth. The Amazon rain forest also has a major impact on weather and climate, regionally and globally.

As splendid as the Amazon region is, there's much more to South America. Like a sharp backbone, the snowcapped Andes run the length of the western side of the continent. These peaks, many over 20,000 feet (6,096 meters) high, make up the second-tallest mountain system on earth. Hiking these mountains is a breathtaking experience—and not just because of the spectacular views. High in the Andes there's so little oxygen in the air that you might feel short of breath, dizzy, or sick to your stomach. This feeling, called altitude sickness, is less common among animals and people who live in the mountains, because they are more adapted to that environment. You, on the other hand, may need to bring extra oxygen, or to take it easy until your body adjusts to the altitude.

If mountain climbing isn't your cup of tea, you can explore South America's other landscapes. You could ride with the *gauchos*, South America's cowboys, as they herd cattle in the *llanos*, the grassy plains of Colombia and Venezuela. You could snorkel with sea lions and penguins over coral reefs in the Galapagos Islands, or fly over spectacular Iguaçu Falls. You could also watch rheas—giant, ostrichlike birds—as they graze on the *pampas*, the grasslands of Argentina. South America not only has these big birds, it has more bird species than any other continent on earth. Bird-watchers boating in the world's biggest wetland, Brazil's Pantanal, which is somewhat like Florida's Everglades, are in for a treat.

A Continent of Contrasts

South America is a continent full of contrasts, both natural and man-made. Chile's Atacama Desert is one of the driest places on earth; some parts of it go without rain for 20 years. Yet the Chocó region of western Colombia has some of the rainiest weather anywhere. South America has cold spots—glaciers in Patagonia and snowy peaks in the Andes. But many of the Andes mountains are also active volcanoes, which emit fiery steam and ash. South America, in fact, has more volcanoes than any other continent.

The people of South America live vastly different lifestyles.
Traffic congestion is not a problem for these Brazilian villagers.

Like the landscape, the lives of South America's people are full of contrast, too. Some people own ranches as big as small states, while others live in shacks. Many South American cities, especially those near the coasts, are densely populated. However, large portions of South America—high mountains, large wetlands, forests, and glaciers—have very few human residents at all. South America has big cities, where people do business among skyscrapers, riding in expensive cars, and using cell phones and fax machines. Yet it also has small villages, only reachable by canoe, where people live age-old lifestyles, depending on the forest for their clothes, medicines, and food.

SOUTH AMERICA: THE BASICS

South America is shaped like an ice-cream cone. It stretches from Point Gallinas in Colombia to Cape Horn, Chile. At its longest, the continent extends about 4,750 miles (7,645 kilometers) from north to south, and at its widest, 3,200 miles (5,150 kilometers) east to west. In the north, South America connects to the country of Panama by a land bridge 30 miles (48 kilometers) wide at its narrowest point. To the south only about 600 miles (1,000 kilometers) of sea lie between South America and Antarctica. The continent includes islands such as the Falkland Islands, the Tierra del Fuego archipelago, and the Galapagos Islands.

South America is surrounded by the Caribbean Sea, the Atlantic Ocean, the Pacific Ocean, and to the south, the Drake Passage, which separates it from Antarctica. Along most of the coast, there is only a narrow continental shelf, which creates a small area of shallows before a quick drop-off to deep ocean. For this reason, South America does not have many good natural harbors, where boats can dock in a sheltered place, out of ocean currents.

MAJOR REGIONS

South America has three main regions: the highlands, the Andes, and the central plains. To the east are the highlands—lands that are higher than average, but not as tall or as jagged as mountains. These broad, ancient lands are divided into two large masses: the Brazilian Highlands and the Guiana Highlands. The Brazilian Highlands are the site of Iguaçu Falls, one of the most spectacular sets of waterfalls on earth.

Lining the western edge of South America are the Andes mountains, which are lofty, snow-covered peaks. These mountains are rising every year, because of volcanic eruptions, and other tectonic activity. The Andes form the southern end of the Cordilleras, the chain of mountains that runs from Alaska to Central America to Tierra del Fuego, at the southern tip of South America.

Sandwiched in between the Andes and the highlands are the central plains, which are low-lying flatlands, mostly river basins. Running through these lowlands are South

Rainbows often appear in the mist below Iguaçu Falls.

America's three main river systems: the Amazon, the Orinoco, and the Río de la Plata. The central plains also contain five important land regions: the llanos, the *selvas*, the *gran chaco*, the pampas, and Patagonia. (*Selvas*, a Spanish word meaning forests, is another term for the Amazon rain forest.)

South America has two major lakes. Lake Maracaibo is located in the lowlands of Venezuela. The other major lake, Lake Titicaca, is high in the Andes, between Peru and Bolivia.

World Records Held by South America

- World's largest river, by volume of water it carries: the Amazon, which discharges an average of 7,000,000 cubic feet (198,000 cubic meters) of water per second at the mouth of the river, where it meets the Atlantic Ocean
- World's highest waterfall: Venezuela's Angel Falls, 3,212 feet (979 meters)
- Highest peak in the Western Hemisphere: Argentina's Aconcagua, 22,831 feet (6,959 meters) above sea level
- Longest mountain system on earth: Andes, 4,500 miles (7,240 kilometers) long
- Second-longest river (after the Nile): Amazon, 4,000 miles (6,450 kilometers)

Statistics and Records for the Continent of South America

- Area: 6,886,000 square miles (17,835,000 square kilometers)
- Population: 329,162,000
- Largest lake: Lake Maracaibo, with a surface area of 5,217 square miles (13,512 square kilometers)
- Lowest point: Valdés Peninsula, Argentina, 131 feet (40 meters) below sea level
- Hottest air temperature ever recorded: Rivadavia, Argentina, 120°F (49°C)

*Spearfishing provides food for this family living on
the Amazon River in Brazil.*

T W O

POSTCARDS FROM SOUTH AMERICA: WEATHER AND CLIMATE

If you were taking a vacation to South America, would you pack a windbreaker or a heavy parka? Would you bring an umbrella for rain or a hat to keep the sun off your head? It would all depend on where you were going, because weather and climate vary among the different regions of South America. Weather conditions can also change dramatically year to year, because of a phenomenon known as El Niño.

GET YOUR BEARINGS

Near Quito, Ecuador, you can straddle the equator, standing with one leg in the Northern Hemisphere and one in the Southern Hemisphere. That's because the equator—the imaginary line that circles the earth's middle—runs through the country of Ecuador. (And that's how the country got its name.) The equator cuts across South America, extending through Brazil to the mouth of the Amazon River. More than two thirds of South America lies in the tropics, the area that hugs the equator.

Being tropical is important because latitude, how close a place is to the North or South Pole or the equator—affects climate. In general, the tropics are warm because the sun shines directly on these regions year round. Each year, the tropics receive more of the sun's energy per square inch (square centimeter) of land than areas nearer the Poles. Brazil's tropical rain forests, for instance, are consistently warm, with an average daily temperature of 86°F (30°C) year round.

Most of South America has relatively mild weather conditions, with fewer temperature extremes than in North America. But there is some variation. The pampas grasslands near Buenos Aires, Argentina, have a daytime temperature of 80°F (27°C) in summer, just like the Amazon. But in winter the pampas turn cool, with average daytime temperatures of only 50°F (10°C).

BE COOL: GO SOUTH

Most of South America is in the Southern Hemisphere, which means in general, the farther south you go, the cooler the climate. (The opposite is true in the Northern Hemisphere, where the weather is generally cooler to the north, toward the North Pole.) Caracas, Venezuela, for instance, is much warmer than Santiago, Chile, which is to the south. Santiago and much of southern South America are located in the subtropical and temperate zones. These regions have variable weather, not as consistently hot as the tropics or as consistently cool as the polar regions. Farther south, in Tierra del Fuego, you will find glaciers, penguins, and much colder weather because it is nearer to the South Pole.

THE WETTEST AND WILDEST PLACE IN SOUTH AMERICA

On the Pacific coast of Colombia and Ecuador lies one of the wettest places in the Western Hemisphere, the Chocó region. Parts of the Chocó receive more than 360 inches (940 centimeters) of rain per year. It is so wet that some of its lowland forests are called wet forests, because they are wetter than rain forests! At higher elevations another forest type, cloud forest, grows.

Cloud forests are almost constantly bathed in fog. Dripping wet tree branches are coated with mosses, orchids, and other epiphytes—plants that perch on other plants. If you can peer through the mist and rain, you might see a black-breasted puffbird, a long-wattled umbrellabird, or one of the twenty-six kinds of hummingbirds that live here. If you are really lucky you might catch sight of the rare spectacled bear.

The Chocó region contains 8,000 to 9,000 plant species, and hundreds of bird species. Scientists believe this small area may have the highest biodiversity of any place on earth. A large percentage of the animals are also endemic, meaning they live nowhere else on earth. Local and international environmentalists are working hard to protect the region and its biodiversity. La Planada, a private nature preserve, protects some of the land. Spectacled bears are being bred in captivity, for release into the wild. And the local Awa Indians are working together with an environmental group, Foundación Herencia Verde, to develop ways to improve farming and to harvest forest products without damaging the forest.

Another Way to Be Cool: Climb Up

If you are flying to Quito, the capitol of Ecuador, bring a light jacket or a sweater for the trip. Even though Quito is close to the equator, it can be cool, because it is at 9,300 feet (2,835 meters) altitude, nestled in the Andes. In South America, indeed anywhere on earth, you will find it is colder at high altitudes. Down in Guayaquil, Ecuador, which is close to sea level, the temperature may be 85°F (29°C), but meanwhile it's only 70°F (21°C) up in Quito, and even cooler higher in the Andes.

South America: Wet and Dry

Air temperatures are not only related to altitude and latitude, they are affected by humidity—the amount of water vapor in the air. Why the connection? Because it takes a lot of energy to heat up water, even water vapor. Humid air is slow to heat up and slow to cool off, so it moderates temperatures. In the Amazon rain forest, moist air acts like a blanket, insulating the region from shifts in temperature. The daily air temperature in the Amazon only varies about 5°F (3°C) from month to month. In contrast, the drier parts of South America can have dramatic changes in temperature, from day to night and season to season. Patagonia, the arid, southernmost region, experiences the biggest seasonal temperature shifts in South America. There is a 36°F (20°C) difference between its warm summers and its cool wintertime temperatures.

'Tis the Season

In tropical South America, the number of hours of daylight changes very little throughout the year. Tropical South America also does not experience a spring, summer, fall, and winter. Instead, areas closest to the equator generally are warm and moist year round. Other tropical areas have one or two wet seasons and one or two dry seasons each year. In a wet season, heavy afternoon rains are common. Rivers may flood. During a dry season, rain is less common or at least not as heavy. Trees in tropical dry forests may drop their leaves during a dry season. But in tropical rain forests, trees generally shed their leaves only a few at a time, throughout the year.

Land, Water, and the Atmosphere

Rainstorms, snowstorms, windstorms, and other weather events take place in the atmosphere—the envelope of air that surrounds the earth. But land and ocean can have a major impact on what happens up in the air. The Andes mountains, for instance, keep Pacific Ocean storms and winds from pushing inland, to the interior of South America. Meanwhile, on the other side of the continent, air flowing over the warm currents in the Atlantic Ocean moves inland, helping the Amazon stay moist. A good example of how the ocean and climate interact can be seen on the coast of Chile, in the Atacama Desert.

THE STRANGE CASE OF THE FOGGY DESERT

If you lived in the Atacama Desert, you might never need an umbrella. You might be twenty years old before you saw your first raindrop fall. Yet you would live much of your life in a cool, wet, fog. The Atacama Desert, which is a 600-mile (968-kilometer) -long ribbon of land in northern Chile, is the most arid place on earth. It receives only ½ inch (13 millimeters) of rain a year, on average. Some parts of it have gone for twenty years without any rain at all!

For a desert the Atacama is rather cool, with an average summer temperature of 66°F (19°C) and 50°F (10°C) in the winter. The Atacama is dry for several reasons. First, the Andes mountains block moist air from the east from reaching the Atacama. In addition, the Atacama is located at a latitude where air masses descend and warm, increasing their capacity to hold water. These air masses, like sponges, dry out the land.

Strangely enough, coastal Atacama is still very foggy, especially in the morning. Fog forms when air passes over the cool waters of the Humboldt Current that flows by the shore. This fog moves inland over the desert, but its moisture rarely condenses to form rain. Instead, the water vapor evaporates into a layer of warm air above.

THE VALLEY OF THE MOON

Plants and animals are scarce in most of the harsh, dry Atacama. Pebbled ground and sand dunes stretch for miles. Salt crystals, left over from lakes that dried up long ago,

How to Harvest Fog

For people living in the Atacama Desert, or in the *altiplano*—a high and dry plateau in Peru—fog is plentiful, but drinking water is scarce. The few rivers that run in these areas do not provide much water. Often that water is polluted by animals, chemicals from mining, and human waste.

Fortunately, in the 1990s, a new program was started to help provide water. With the assistance of the International Development Research Center of Canada, people in the altiplano and Atacama erected huge nets that catch the fog that floats past. It takes an estimated 10 million droplets of fog to form one single water droplet. But there is plenty of fog to go around.

In *The Living Earth Book of Deserts,* author Susan Arritt describes the nets as standing 13 feet (4 meters) high and stretching 40 feet (12 meters) wide. Fog condenses on the nets and runs down into buckets and pipes. One net can collect 45 gallons (170 liters) of water in a day. The nets provide villagers in both the Atacama and the altiplano with clean water for drinking, cooking, and other needs.

Fog nets—a recent addition in parts of the Atacama Desert—help to provide much-needed water.

make the reddish soil sparkle with a white crust. At the base of steep cliffs that line the coast, a few small plants grow, watered by spray from crashing waves. But crops can be grown only with water pumped up into fields from the few rivers in the Atacama. In fact, the Atacama is so arid that most of the rivers there dry up before they reach the ocean; only the Loa River makes it all the way to the sea.

Animal life is scarce in the driest parts of the Atacama. But the salt lakes, which can be moist after rains, attract large flocks of flamingos. Flamingos turn their bills upside down and swish them in the water in order to filter out edible algae. Just how dry and barren is the Atacama? One area, called the Valley of the Moon, is so lifeless that American scientists from the National Aeronautics and Space Administration (NASA) used this place to test a robot designed to explore other planets and moons!

MIRACLE IN THE ATACAMA

In 1997 something extraordinary happened. The Atacama Desert bloomed. A land that is usually dry and lifeless—just sand and pebbles, really—almost overnight became a field of colorful flowers. People living in the desert could hardly believe it. It seemed like *un milagro*, a miracle! Sprouting out of the sand were flowers that naturalists did not know still existed in the desert, or that had not been seen for years. Apparently, the seeds had been lying dormant in the soil for decades, some for perhaps a half century. The flowers grew and bloomed because in 1997 the Atacama received several inches of rain, much more than normal. These rain showers were caused by a particularly strong El Niño, an important weather phenomenon that occurs every four to seven years.

EL NIÑO: WHEN THE WEATHER GOES WILD

The El Niño event of 1997–1998 did much more than bring rain to the Atacama. It had a broad array of effects worldwide. There were floods in California, tornadoes and wildfires in Florida, warm weather in Chicago, and droughts in Indonesia and Australia. South America was hard hit, with torrential rains in Peru and Ecuador, which resulted in deadly floods and mud slides that washed away towns and destroyed highways. In Peru, 59 bridges collapsed. Three hundred people were killed. Hundreds of thousands more had to leave their homes.

WHAT IS EL NIÑO?

An El Niño is a natural shift in climatic conditions, which occurs periodically. It happens when a huge mass of warm water forms off the coast of Peru and Ecuador, where there is normally a cold current. In December 1997 the pool of warm water stretched over an area 1½ times the size of the United States. This warm water heated and moistened the

Seeds lying dormant in desert soil for perhaps as long as 50 years bloomed in the Atacama as a result of increased rainfall caused by El Niño.

air above it, developing storms that moved eastward, pummeling the Americas, from California to Peru.

Normally—in non–El Niño years—steady winds, called trade winds, push surface water in the Pacific Ocean westward toward the coast of Asia. Cool water from deep in the ocean then comes to the surface near Peru, to fill in where the warm water was. The cold-water flow is called the Humboldt Current.

In El Niño years, the trade winds weaken and the water is not pushed westward. Instead, it pools up, off the coast of Ecuador and Peru. This change in the ocean causes a radical flip in weather worldwide. Suddenly, southeast Asia has droughts, because it no longer has the warm water and warm air near its coast. Meanwhile, Peru, Ecuador, and California get torrential rains. But the effects reach farther still. Like the wake of a

El Niño brought destruction to some areas. In Ecuador, streets were covered by floodwaters.

motorboat felt all over a lake, the shift of warm water in the Pacific Ocean affects the weather even far away.

EL NIÑO AND ANCHOVIES

In normal years, non–El Niño years, the fishing near Peru is outstanding. Cold, oxygen-rich, nutrient-rich water from the ocean bottom comes to the surface, fertilizing floating ocean plants. These tiny plants, called phytoplankton, are eaten by zooplankton—tiny floating ocean animals. The zooplankton are eaten by fish. The fish, in turn, are eaten by people and seabirds. Because of this ocean food chain, Peru has one of the world's biggest fishing industries. Anchovies, which are small fish caught off Peru's shores, become fertilizer and food for livestock such as cows, pigs, and chickens. (The chicken you eat may have been fed ground-up Peruvian anchovies.)

All this changes every four to seven years, when an El Niño occurs. The cold, nutrient-

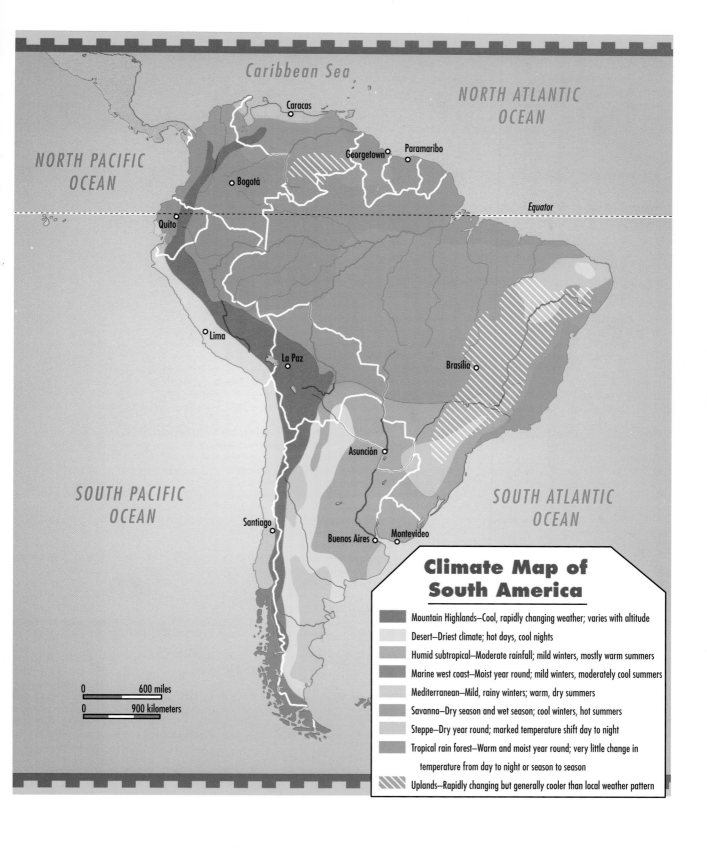

Caribbean Sea

NORTH ATLANTIC OCEAN

NORTH PACIFIC OCEAN

Caracas

Georgetown   Paramaribo

Bogotá

Equator

Quito

Lima

La Paz

Brasília

SOUTH PACIFIC OCEAN

Asunción

SOUTH ATLANTIC OCEAN

Santiago

Buenos Aires   Montevideo

0   600 miles
0   900 kilometers

Climate Map of South America

Mountain Highlands—Cool, rapidly changing weather; varies with altitude

Desert—Driest climate; hot days, cool nights

Humid subtropical—Moderate rainfall; mild winters, mostly warm summers

Marine west coast—Moist year round; mild winters, moderately cool summers

Mediterranean—Mild, rainy winters; warm, dry summers

Savanna—Dry season and wet season; cool winters, hot summers

Steppe—Dry year round; marked temperature shift day to night

Tropical rain forest—Warm and moist year round; very little change in temperature from day to night or season to season

Uplands—Rapidly changing but generally cooler than local weather pattern

THE GALAPAGOS ISLANDS

In the Galapagos Islands, you can see wildlife at close range. A giant tortoise or blue-footed booby may stand in your path. Frigate birds have been known to perch on boats, and mockingbirds have even landed on people's heads! Underwater, while snorkeling, you may see Galapagos penguins hunting fish or a marine iguana eating seaweed. A sea lion may tug at the flippers on your feet. The reason visitors can get so close to Galapagos animals is that no large predators have lived on the islands, until recently. Because large predators have not been a threat for very long, the animals have not developed a fear of large animals, or a habit of fleeing from them. (Unfortunately, this "tameness" made it easy for sailors to slaughter thousands of tortoises and seabirds in the early 1800s.)

The 19 islands in the Galapagos group lie 600 miles (965 kilometers) west of Ecuador. Although the Galapagos Islands are near the equator, the cold Humboldt Current makes air temperatures very comfortable, in the 70s°F (low 20s°C). Seabirds such as frigate birds, swallow-tailed gulls, lava gulls, red-footed boobies, blue-footed boobies, masked boobies, and waved albatrosses nest on the islands. Tortoises, iguanas, and mockingbirds vary slightly from island to island. Many of the animals in the Galapagos are endemic.

The Galapagos Islands are famous for their 13 species of finches, mentioned by Charles Darwin in his book *The Origin of Species by Means of Natural Selection*. Charles Darwin, who voyaged to the Galapagos on the H.M.S. *Beagle* in the 1830s, is known for his formulation of the idea of evolution and natural selection. He used some of what he learned in the Galapagos to support his ideas.

Today the Galapagos Islands are also the site of a long-term research study of evolution and natural selection. Every year for two decades, scientists Peter and Rosemary

rich current disappears, and the Peruvians' fishing success suddenly plummets. Peruvian fishermen were the ones who named the phenomenon El Niño, meaning "the child," because they usually felt its effects near Christmas, the birthday of the Christ Child.

THE EL NIÑO OF THE CENTURY

The El Niño of 1997–1998 was called the El Niño of the century because the climate shift was so strong. Fish were so scarce near Chile that confused, starving pelicans invaded the streets of Arica, Chile, blocking traffic in the town. Meanwhile, unusually warm ocean waters caused coral near the Galapagos Islands to bleach, meaning it turned white. This bleaching occurred because the coral animals ejected the algae that normally

Grant have measured the beaks of the finches on Daphne Major, one of the Galapagos Islands. What difference does the size of a bird's beak make? Different-size beaks are better for cracking open and eating different kinds of seeds. Droughts, heavy rains, and other environmental conditions change which seeds are more plentiful. This, in turn, has affected which birds, with which size beaks, have survived and reproduced. The Grants' study measurements showed that some generations of birds have had larger beaks, and some generations have had lots of birds with smaller beaks. In this way, they have documented evolution and natural selection occurring over time. Their study, one of the most important documenting evolution and natural selection, is described in the best-selling book *The Beak of the Finch.*

Giant tortoises are only one of the sights that bring tourists to the Galapagos Islands.

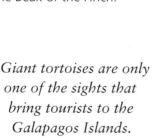

live inside them. (Bleaching is very damaging to coral reefs, although the corals can sometimes recover.)

Effects of El Niño were felt elsewhere in South America. While heavy rains flooded Peruvian homes, a terrible drought hit the Amazon region. The forest became so dry that it burned easily, and forest fires raged unchecked, causing some of the most widespread damage ever. In this unusual year, it was evident that the ocean, the air, and the land do indeed interact to create the weather and climate that affect people's lives.

Rapids tumble at the base of a snow-covered volcano in Chile.

THREE

NATURAL HIGHS: THE ANDES AND THE HIGHLANDS

For thousands of years the people of the Andes have worshipped the mountains. That is not surprising, considering that mountains affect so many aspects of their lives. The mountains, interacting with clouds, help bring rain. The mountains, many of which are volcanoes, can also erupt, burying towns in ash, lava, and mud. Yet that same volcanic ash that can bring tragedy to a village also fertilizes the soil, making the growth of crops possible. The geologic activity that formed the Andes has even created reservoirs of valuable minerals, such as gold, silver, copper, and tin.

THE LOWDOWN ON THE HIGH ANDES

The Andes mountains are the longest mountain system on any continent, stretching more than 4,500 miles (7,200 kilometers) from northern Venezuela to Tierra del Fuego. They snake through seven countries: Venezuela, Colombia, Ecuador, Peru, Chile, Bolivia, and Argentina. At times the mountains divide into several parallel mountain chains, and at other times they narrow to one. But the entire mountain system is never more than about 500 miles (806 kilometers) wide.

The Himalayas of Asia have some peaks higher than those in the Andes. But for sheer number of tall mountains, the Andes win—with the most peaks more than 10,000 feet (3,049 meters) high. North of Santiago, Chile, lies the highest Andean peak, Aconcagua, which is more than 4 miles (almost 7 kilometers) high. People who climb to the tops of these mountains must carefully plan their trips, allowing time for their bodies to adjust to the altitude. Near the summits of these mountains, the air contains so little oxygen, that many people, unaccustomed to the thin air, can become very ill and even die.

MOUNTAINS ON THE MOVE

Immense and towering, mountains can seem unchangeable, dependable, and permanent. But the opposite is true, especially in the Andes, where mountains smoke, hillsides slide, and earthquakes shake the soil. Many Andean mountains are active volcanoes. Steam and ash may rise from their peaks. Geysers—fountains of water and steam heated by the molten magma underground—explode out of crevices in the ground. Earthquakes, which can be connected to volcanic activity, are common in the Andes, too. Each year, about 2,500 noticeable earthquakes, almost half the world's total, occur in the Andes.

If you lived in a valley in the Andes, you might never notice the mountains rising. A volcano might not erupt in your lifetime. But then again, it might. That is why the

ANCIENT TREASURE OF THE ANDES

Treasure, according to Webster's dictionary, is something of great worth or value. The Andes certainly have great worth, in their rich soils, their beauty, their wildlife, their people, and their fascinating cultures. But other kinds of treasure—gold, silver, tin, copper, and sulfur—have also shaped the Andes' history.

In 1545, or so the story goes, a man built a campfire on Cerro Rico, a mountain in the Bolivian Andes. The heat of his fire made white liquid drip from nearby rock. He had found a deposit of silver. Cerro Rico, which means "rich hill," was soon mined for silver, gold, and tin. Spanish explorers, after conquering the Inca Empire, shipped tons of South American silver and gold back to Europe.

Over the last four and half centuries, miners have endured cold, hunger, fatigue, cave-ins, and backbreaking work while toiling in the tunnels that worm their way through the mountains. To help endure the terrible conditions, miners chew coca, a leaf that gives a mild narcotic rush. (The illegal drug cocaine is made from coca leaves, but cocaine is much, much stronger than the coca leaves the miners chew.) Mining accidents and respiratory disease caused by mining dust have killed many miners. Most of the rich veins of silver, gold, copper, and tin in the Andes have been mined already. But mining is still an important industry in Bolivia. What is left to mine are low-grade minerals, mixed in with other rock, making it costly and difficult to extract them.

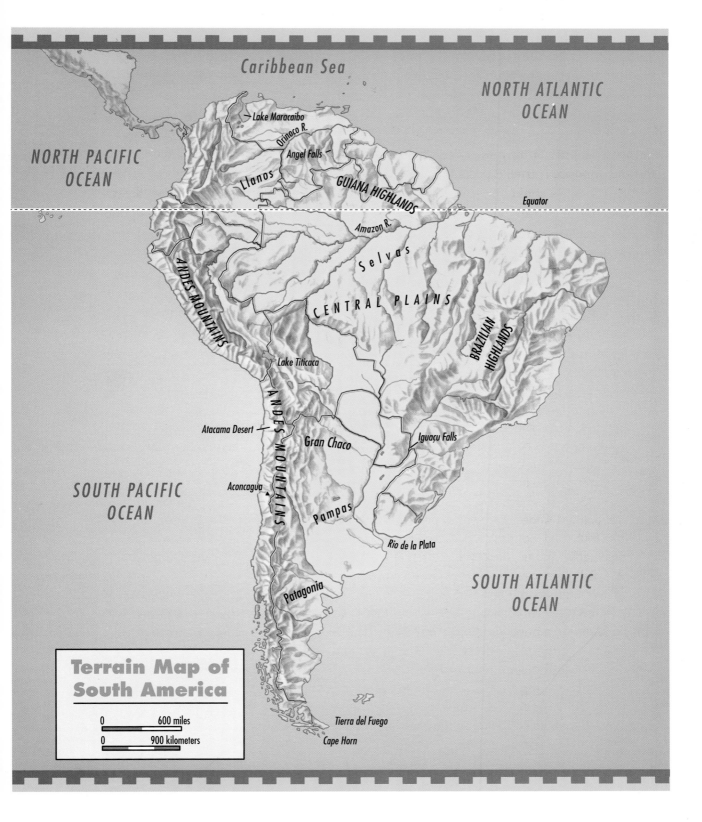

Caribbean Sea

NORTH ATLANTIC
OCEAN

NORTH PACIFIC
OCEAN

Lake Maracaibo

Orinoco R.

Angel Falls

Llanos

GUIANA HIGHLANDS

Equator

Amazon R.

Selvas

CENTRAL PLAINS

ANDES MOUNTAINS

BRAZILIAN
HIGHLANDS

Lake Titicaca

ANDES MOUNTAINS

Atacama Desert

Gran Chaco

Iguaçu Falls

SOUTH PACIFIC
OCEAN

Aconcagua ▲

Pampas

Rio de la Plata

SOUTH ATLANTIC
OCEAN

Patagonia

**Terrain Map of
South America**

| 0 | 600 miles |
| 0 | 900 kilometers |

Tierra del Fuego

Cape Horn

people in the village of Latacunga, Ecuador, practice volcano drills once a year. When sirens sound, children leave school, adults leave work, and everyone in town climbs the highest hill in the region. The hill is the safest place to be in case of a volcanic eruption, because an eruption could cause mud to flow into nearby lowlands. A volcano can trigger mud slides because the heat of the volcano rapidly melts glaciers covering it. In minutes, a melting glacier can turn a mountainside to mud that can bury a town. Such a disaster occurred in Armero, Colombia, on November 13, 1985. Nevado del Ruiz, a volcano 30 miles (48 kilometers) from town, erupted, melting the mountain's glacier and creating a lahar, a liquid landslide of mud, water, and ash. The lahar rushed down the mountainside, burying the town 20 feet (6 meters) deep in only 15 minutes. More than 23,000 people were killed. After the disaster, people rebuilt their homes. But the volcano erupted again in 1991 and 1996, killing tens of thousands more people.

UP GO THE ANDES

Tall mountains are made in three different ways. One continent may ram into another, thrusting up mountains such as the Himalayas. Or magma may spurt out of the ground from natural hot spots in the earth, then cool and build up, forming volcanic mountains such as the Hawaiian Islands. A third kind of mountain building occurs in the Andes.

The Andes began forming about 180 million years ago, when the tectonic plate beneath the Pacific Ocean collided with South America. This collision crumpled the continent, setting in motion the formation of the Andes. Today, the Andes are rising. In a process called subduction, the seafloor of the Pacific Ocean is actually plunging underneath South America as South America moves westward, riding on the American Plate. The plunging slab of seafloor is being compressed and heated, causing it and overlying rock to melt. This molten rock builds up, and eventually explodes out of Andean volcanoes. The magma that shoots out eventually cools and forms rock that builds the mountains higher. In this way, the motion of tectonic plates continues lifting the Andes higher.

This is a simple explanation of what is happening in the Andes. More and more, scientists are discovering that the Andes are a very complex mountain system, and different portions may have been formed in slightly different ways.

FROM BASE TO PEAK

From the base of the Andes mountains to their peaks, there's a noticeable change in climate, plants, and animals. Near the foot of the mountains is *tierra calienta*, the "hot land," where lowland rain forests occur, and farmers grow fields of tobacco, bananas, sugarcane, corn, and cacao beans, from which chocolate is made. Farther up is *tierra templada*, the "temperate zone," which has cooler weather, more evergreen trees, and good conditions for growing coffee beans. Still farther up is *tierra fria*, the "cold zone." Cloud forests grow in the lower part of the tierra fria. Where the land is cleared, people grow bamboo, potatoes, and wheat, often on terraces, staircaselike rows built for growing crops on steep slopes. On the upper part of the tierra fria, where trees do not grow, is a grassland called *paramo*. Andean condors soar in the skies, while llamas and alpacas graze below. Above the tierra fria is the most forbidding, coldest part of the Andes, where snow stays on the ground year round.

LAKE TITICACA AND THE ALTIPLANO

Lake Titicaca is so deep that Jacques Cousteau, the famous explorer and environmentalist, once studied it by diving down in a small submarine. Titicaca, the second-largest lake in South America, is also the highest major lake in the world, at an altitude of 12,500 feet (3,810 meters). Titicaca lies in the altiplano, which means "high plateau," a region between two mountain ranges that are part of the Andes. Rain and melting snow from the surrounding mountains pour into more than 25 rivers that run into Lake Titicaca. Waterbirds such as silvery grebes, giant Andean coots, and puna ibises can be found on the lake. Flamingos feed on salt flats not far away. With crystal blue waters and beautiful islands, Lake Titicaca has been revered as a sacred place for thousands of years. The local people once regularly used canoes made of bundles of reeds, a grasslike marsh plant. They even constructed floating islands of reeds and built houses on them!

Natives of the Lake Titicaca region have used reeds to create many things, including canoes.

ONE POTATO, TWO POTATO, THREE POTATO...

If you like French fries, mashed potatoes, or hashed browns, you have the people of the Andes to thank. The wild potato plant originated in the Andes, where the native people developed it into a crop plant, over thousands of years. The Incas, who lived in the Andes 600 years ago, freeze-dried potatoes by leaving potatoes out in the cold mountain air, then squeezing the water out of them. When this process was repeated several times, a potato could then be safely stored for several years! These days you may find 40 or more kinds of potatoes in a Peruvian marketplace—blue potatoes, red potatoes, white potatoes, orange potatoes—all with different tastes and textures. As many as 600 kinds of potatoes can be found throughout the Andes. (The sweet potato, however, is another plant entirely, which may have originated in the Caribbean.)

CAMELS OF THE ANDES

Hiking in the Andes, you may meet a camel. But do not expect it to have any humps. South America's wild camels, the vicuña and the guanaco, are smaller, more slender, and less lumpy than their Asian cousins. Vicuñas are the smallest camels, only 36 inches (91 centimeters) high at the shoulder and weighing only 110 pounds (50 kilograms). They are featherweights compared with the dromedary camels of Egypt, which can weigh 1,200 pounds (550 kilograms)!

Both vicuñas and guanacos have thick, woolly coats, which keep them warm in the high, cold mountains. Unusually big hearts and large lungs are adaptations that both animals have evolved to help them gather a lot of oxygen at high altitudes, where the amount of oxygen in the air is low. Herds of vicuñas and guanacos live wild, grazing on grass, from high in the Andes down to the lower plains. But over thousands of years, wild guanacos have been bred to form two types of domestic animal: the alpaca and the llama. Alpacas and llamas are herded in the Andes, where they are used for wool, meat, and transportation.

CONSERVING CAMELS

Vicuña fur is perhaps the softest and silkiest in the world. Only Inca royalty were allowed to wear it. The vicuñas were protected by law in the time of the Inca, when there may have been more than a million vicuñas roaming free in South America. But then the Spanish *conquistadores* came in the 1500s, the Inca Empire collapsed, and people began

Vicuña populations, once in decline, are increasing in Peru and elsewhere in South America.

hunting the vicuña for meat and hides. These slender camels almost became extinct. By the 1960s there were only a few thousand left.

Fortunately, the story of the vicuña is a happy one, because they are now protected once again. The people of the *puna*, a windswept tableland or basin where vicuña live, have returned to their tradition of protecting the wild vicuña and annually harvesting their wool. Each spring, local people round up the animals and shear their wool with electric shavers. Then the animals are released, unharmed. Their wool regrows. Meanwhile, the people can sell the wool they have harvested, which brings in almost an entire year's income for them. The number of vicuña has been increasing every year; there are at least 600,000 today.

SOUTH AMERICA'S OTHER HIGH POINTS: THE BRAZILIAN HIGHLANDS AND GUIANA HIGHLANDS

The Andes are not the only high places in South America. More than one third of South America's surface is made up of the Brazilian Highlands and the Guiana Highlands. These tremendous masses of ancient rock are very durable, but in some places, softer rock has eroded away, forming dramatic plateaus—tall, broad, tablelike landforms that stand up above the rest of the land. High hills and deep valleys make travel through the highlands region difficult. The Guiana Highlands are home to Angel Falls, and the *tepuis*, which have remarkable scenery.

REMOTE, RARE, TOWERING TEPUIS

If you want to go where almost no one has gone before, and see plants and animals that few have seen, you might try exploring Venezuela's tepuis. Tepuis are towering sandstone mesas—tablelike rock formations as much as 9,094 feet (2,772 meters) tall. More than a hundred tepuis rise out of the llanos and rain forests of southeastern Venezuela. Shrouded in mist, with steep cliff sides, the tops of tepuis are hard to reach. So the tepuis have not been farmed, grazed, or inhabited by people. Now most tepuis are preserved in Canaima National Park, which is visited by tourists and scientists who take helicopters to reach the tops of the tepuis. But many parts of the tepuis remain unexplored.

Some tepuis are like islands in a sea of savanna. Plants and animals that have long ago died out elsewhere survive on the tops of these mesas. For years, explorers dreamed of finding dinosaurs surviving up on these tepuis, isolated from the rest of the world. So far dinosaurs have not been found, but what scientists have found are hundreds of plant species that live nowhere else on earth. Isolated up on these tepuis, animals and plants have evolved separately from organisms in the surrounding lands.

Covered with clouds, and strange black rock formations, the tepuis are unique. Walking on the tepuis gives you a feeling of being somewhere remote, ancient, and mysterious. For starters, the underlying sandstone is 1.8 billion years old. Some canyons have ground that sparkles pink and white because it is made of quartz crystals. Angel Falls, the world's highest waterfall, cascades more than 3,000 feet (914 meters) down the sandstone cliffs of Auyan-tepui. (Angel Falls got its name from Jimmy Angel, a pilot who

Riches under Lake Maracaibo

In Venezuela, near a northeastern extension of the Andes, is a hot, humid region and a tremendous lake. The lake, Lake Maracaibo, is the continent's largest, with a surface area of 5,217 square miles (13,512 square kilometers). Fed by more than 135 different rivers, Lake Maracaibo is a good port for ships, because it is connected to the Caribbean through the Gulf of Venezuela. But Maracaibo's biggest attraction is hidden beneath the lake water.

Every day more than 10,000 oil wells pump petroleum out from under Lake Maracaibo. To service the wells, and carry the oil, 38,710 miles (24,000 kilometers) of pipes have been laid under the lake. Deep channels have been dredged in the shallow lake bottom so that oil tankers can move through the lake. Through the new channels, ocean water is entering the lake, making it saltier. Some of the lake's native animals are decreasing in number because they cannot survive in the salty water.

Pollution is a big problem in Lake Maracaibo. Human sewage, pesticides, fertilizers, and industrial wastes all run into the lake. The possibility of an oil spill is also a major concern. But the government, environmental groups, and private citizens are working hard to solve these problems. They are building new sewage treatment plants to clean the water, and setting up programs to safeguard against oil spills.

accidentally found Angel Falls when he was flying around Venezuela, searching for gold in 1935.) Jimmy Angel may have found the falls, but there is still much left to explore about the tepuis.

Many of the tepuis have hardly any soil at all, yet plants such as lichens, mosses, and even orchids survive in clumps and patches. Insectivorous plants, such as sundews and pitcher plants, trap insects and digest them to get nitrogen the soils lack. Almost every major expedition to the tepuis discovers a new plant species. Perhaps one day you could be the scientist who finds a new plant!

FALLING FOR IGUAÇU

More than 2 miles (3.2 kilometers) wide, with 275 separate waterfalls, Iguaçu Falls is one of South America's major tourist sites. It is also the widest set of waterfalls in the world. Shared by Argentina and Brazil, the falls cascade off the eroded cliffs of the Brazilian plateau, and pour into the Iguaçu River. Water plunges about 240 feet (about 73 meters) down some of the Iguaçu's Falls, which are 50 percent taller than Niagara

Falls. Iguaçu is a native name meaning "great waters," and it certainly describes the place. Rainbows shine out of the mist made by the falling water. Colorful orchids grow on trees and cliffs. Parrots, howler monkeys, and coatimundis—raccoonlike mammals—live in the surrounding rain forests of Iguaçu Falls National Park. Here, as in the Andes, it is easy to feel awed by the wonders of South America's natural landscape.

Large flightless birds called rheas can be seen in the pampas and in the plains of Patagonia.

FOUR

FROM THE PLAINS TO PATAGONIA

Where can you find the world's largest rodents, living in galloping, grazing herds? Where can you see giant flightless birds running, or storks and egrets rising up like clouds? All these animals live on South America's central plains, which lie between the Brazilian Highlands and the Andes mountains. These low-lying lands are drained by the continent's great river systems: the Orinoco, the Amazon, and the Río de la Plata.

Five major areas make up the plains: the llanos, the gran chaco, the pampas, Patagonia, and the selvas. The selvas are discussed further in chapter 5. In this chapter we linger in South America's other lowlands: landscapes with open spaces, waving grasses, thorny shrubs, vast wetlands, and a wide array of wild creatures.

SALUTE TO SAVANNAS

Imagine a place where grasses and small shrubs stretch for miles, with only scattered trees. This is savanna—a biome common in the tropics, and also a place of weather extremes. During the dry season, from November through April, a savanna can be so dry that plants wither and animals starve. Yet during the wet season, from May to October, in low-lying savannas, the land may flood, filling with fish, waterbirds, and caimans—relatives of alligators. The savanna biome is widespread in South America. Two of the major savanna regions are the llanos of Colombia and Venezuela and the gran chaco in Bolivia, Paraguay, and Argentina.

Twice as big as Nevada, the llanos lies just east of the Andes mountains in Venezuela and Colombia. A low-lying plain drained by the Orinoco River, the llanos is home to birds, deer, and jaguars. But most of all, the llanos is full of brahmans, a humpbacked, sturdy breed of cattle, herded by *llaneros*—the local cowboys.

Poor soil, floods, and droughts make savannas difficult places to grow crops. For the same reasons, trees only grow in small stands, along rivers, and on higher ground. But cattle ranching is a successful business in the llanos, and ecotourism is becoming important, too.

Ecotourism—tourism that brings people to see wildlife and natural features—is working well on large ranches in Venezuela. By limiting hunting on their lands, ranchers have allowed wildlife to thrive. These ranches are home to howler monkeys, pumas, iguanas, vultures, and capybaras—piglike rodents. In dry seasons cattle graze on land that in the wet season floods, attracting waterbirds such as spoonbills, scarlet ibises, and

A group of capybaras pauses at the edge of a stream while searching for water plants to eat.

storks. Wildlife guides with canoes or motorboats move through the flooded areas, showing tourists hoatzins, sun bitterns, and other birds.

Ranchers occasionally lose cows to the jaguars, which attack cattle. But the broad range of wildlife in the llanos has its advantages, too. Birds, such as egrets, caracaras, and cattle tyrants actually eat the ticks and fleas off the cattle, helping to keep them healthy!

Animals That Aren't All Wet

Llanos animals have remarkable adaptations to the wet and dry seasons. In the dry season snakes wriggle down into the mud, hibernating until the rain returns. Some frogs lie low, forming hard, watertight cases around their bodies in order to stay wet until the dry season is over. Strange-looking fish called lungfish have a special air bladder that helps them breathe air and live in mud after a pond or river has dried up!

One Big Rodent

Weighing as much as some adult humans, the 110-pound (50-kilogram) capybara definitely tips the scales as the world's largest rodent. On South America's savannas, these grass eaters are also the biggest native grazers. Capybaras are close relatives of rats, squirrels, and beavers. Yet they actually look more like small pigs, but with squared off snouts and partially webbed feet. Abundant in the llanos of Venezuela, capybaras live in herds. They often swim in rivers, streams, and ponds, feeding on water plants.

Gran Chaco

Like the llanos, the gran chaco is a low-lying, relatively flat region. It was formed by sediments that eroded from high in the Andes then flowed down rivers and deposited in the lowlands. Lying in Bolivia, Paraguay, and Argentina, the gran chaco is a mixture of savanna and thorn forest.

Driving through the chaco, you'll reach an area where the roads run out, and a place the local people call *El Impenetrable* begins. Soon, it will be clear to you what they are describing: acres and acres of interlocking, thorny shrubs that make the region almost impenetrable—almost impossible to walk through. In summer the air is dry and hot, so bring water for any adventures in the gran chaco. You will also need to watch out for thorns on the road because they have been known to puncture auto tires!

Growing in the gran chaco are some very strange trees. One is the *quebracho*, which has extremely hard wood; its name means "axbreaker!" Another tree, the *palo borracho*, or bottle tree, has a pear-shaped trunk that stores up water for use during drought. The chaco habitat, and nearby marshes and savannas, are preserved in Parque Nacional

Large flights of flamingos sometimes fill the skies over Argentina.

Chaco, near the town of Resistencia, Argentina, and in Parque Nacional Defensores del Chaco, near Filadelfia, Paraguay. Pumas, jaguars, and peccaries—wild pigs—can be found in these areas. There are also resident tapirs—donkey-size animals that look a bit like pigs but are really more closely related to rhinoceroses.

PAMPAS: HOME OF REALLY BIG BIRDS

What's brown, 5 feet (1.5 meters) tall, and has feathers but can't fly? It's the rhea, the biggest of the American birds. Rheas, also called ñandús, look a lot like ostriches. They live in the pampas of Argentina and Uruguay. They also inhabit the dry grasslands of Patagonia. These three-toed birds eat seeds and insects. In flocks of 20 or more, they often travel with deer or guanacos. (Interestingly, ostriches, which live in Africa, travel in mixed herds, too—with antelopes and zebra.) Male rheas, like male ostriches, incubate the eggs and herd the young, caring for them until they can fend for themselves.

The pampas, where rheas roam, fan out from the coastal city of Buenos Aires in the Río de la Plata river system, where the Uruguay and Paraná rivers meet. Mostly grassland, the pampas are broken up by only a few hills and sand dunes. Much of the pampas

42

is divided into large cattle ranches, known in Spanish as *estancias*. Cowboys, called *gauchos*, herd cattle and horses. But like the prairies of North America, the pampas are also a good agricultural area, especially for wheat, which does not need much water during its growing season. Even with the farming and cattle ranching, there is still wildlife on the pampas. You might see armadillos crossing a road, clouds of flamingos and spoonbills rising off a field, or burrowing owls standing atop their burrows. On top of fence posts, *horneros*, which means "oven birds," construct clay nests that look like traditional clay ovens.

PATAGONIA'S CHILLY COASTS

Patagonia, the southern tip of South America, is a cool, rocky, windswept place. Encompassing southern Argentina and southern Chile, it extends to Tierra del Fuego—a group of islands shared by both countries. The western side of Patagonia contains the southern end of the Andes. From the Andes, a dry plateau stretches east toward the Atlantic Ocean.

Part of a Patagonian glacier breaks off and falls into the sea, in a process called "calving."

More than 6,000 square miles (15,540 square kilometers) of Patagonia is covered by glaciers, slow-moving rivers of ice. Over thousands of years these glaciers have carved out fjords—steep-cliffed valleys that have flooded with seawater. Patagonia's fjords may remind you of coastal Norway, Iceland, or Alaska; those landscapes were affected by glaciers, too. If you ride a boat through the Strait of Magellan—the waterway that passes between Tierra del Fuego and mainland South America—you can see blue glaciers hanging over the water. Occasionally the ice cracks, dropping icebergs into the water below. Water melting from glaciers cascades over cliffs and pours into fjords, turning the water an intense light green. Seabirds such as black-browed albatrosses and imperial cormorants skim the water for fish.

Patagonia also has penguins. On Magdalena Island, just off the coast of Patagonia, Magellanic penguins waddle over beaches, raising their fluffy gray chicks in burrows in dry soil. In southern South America, colonies of penguins and other seabirds gather to nest on coasts and islands. So many of these birds gather close together that their droppings, called guano, can really pile up. The guano is even mined and sold for fertilizer!

WINDY AND WILD: INLAND PATAGONIA

Farther inland, Patagonia's scenery is different. It's brown and windswept. The Andes block Pacific moisture from reaching Patagonia, making this area very dry. It receives less than 10 inches (25 centimeters) of rain each year—about as much as a desert. In ice-free areas grow tufts of grass and widely spaced shrubs. Sheep and cattle graze on large ranches. Farming is only possible near rivers, where water is available for irrigation.

Patagonia's crown jewel is Torres del Paine, a national park 100 miles (160 kilometers) from Puerto Natales, Chile. The park is a great place to see the native animals, such as hares, foxes, guanacos, and 105 species of birds, including flamingos, condors, parrots, crested caracaras, and rheas. The *torres*, meaning "towers," that give the park its name are strangely shaped peaks surrounded by breathtakingly beautiful lakes.

SOMETHING STRANGE ABOUT SOUTH AMERICA

Africa has zebras, giraffes, rhinoceroses, elephants, wildebeests, and many other large herbivores—animals that eat plants. But South America, which has savannas and grasslands like Africa, has no really large native herbivores. South America, in fact, does not have many big land animals at all. The largest is the tapir, a forest-dwelling, 400-pound (180-kilogram) animal that looks a little like a pig. It's heavy, but not that heavy compared with an African elephant, which can weigh 6 tons (5.4 metric tons)!

Still, size is not everything. Wildlife watching in South America is spectacular, especially in the world's largest wetland, the Pantanal. This South Dakota–size region, cov-

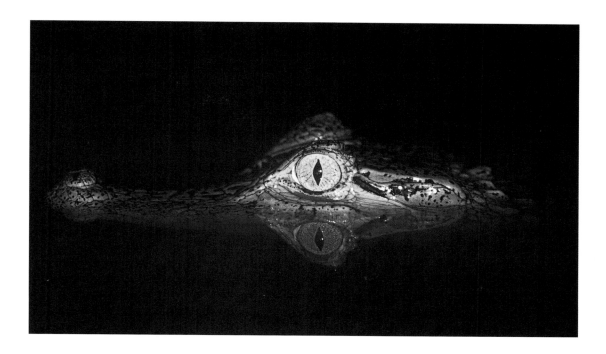

The caimans of South America are closely related to alligators found in the southeastern United States.

ering parts of Brazil, Paraguay, and Bolivia, combines wildlife from South America's dry savannas with wildlife from the wet Amazon. Between January and March, in the wet season, the region floods, forming a patchwork of streams, lakes, ponds, and islands. Spoonbills, capybaras, tapirs, wood storks, snail kites, maned wolves, marsh deer, giant anteaters, and more than 650 kinds of fish live in the region. Even hyacinth macaws, rare birds endangered by the international pet trade, are fairly easy to see in the Pantanal.

If you're a gator fan, you will love the Pantanal, which has 10 million or so caimans, relatives of alligators. Go out at night and shine a flashlight on the water, and you will see their glowing eyes. Then you will have no doubt that the central plains of South America have plenty of wildlife worth watching—plus some wildlife that may be watching you!

Flowering vines add bright color to the moist green foliage of the Amazon.

FIVE

AWESOME AMAZONIA

If you've heard shocking and colorful stories about the creatures of the Amazon, they may very well be true. Electric eels—snakelike fish that stun their prey with electric shocks—inhabit the Amazon River. So do neon tetras, the brightly colored "fighting" fish you see in pet stores in the United States. Other amazing Amazon inhabitants include parrots, jaguars, and giant anteaters, which slurp up ants with their 24-inch (60-centimeter)-long tongues! Plant lovers would be content in the Amazon, too, sighting colorful orchids, bromeliads, and strangler figs and other trees. Insect enthusiasts could spend years searching for hidden insects that look like twigs, thorns, and leaves. All these plants and animals live in a habitat that encompasses a river and rain forest unlike any other on earth.

TAKE A TRIP DOWN THE AMAZON

If you go kayaking or canoeing down the Amazon River, you might be amazed at how it changes along its route. High in the Peruvian Andes, the Amazon begins as an icy-cold mountain spring. The official source of the Amazon River is about 100 miles (160 kilometers) from the Pacific Ocean, at an elevation of 18,363 feet (5,597 meters). From there the river rapidly descends, cascading over waterfalls and churning through deep canyons during its first 500 miles (about 800 kilometers).

As the Amazon River flows toward the Atlantic Ocean, it slows and widens, becoming warm, sluggish, and flat. By the time it reaches Iquitos, Peru, the Amazon is wide enough for huge, ocean-going ships! Tremendous 276-pound (125-kilogram) fish called *pirarucu* live in the rivers. So do the most famous of Amazonian fish—piranhas. Fortunately, most piranha species, despite their flesh-tearing teeth, are harmless to people. But black piranhas can be dangerous. When the water recedes after floods, these fish can be stranded in natural pools. When these pools begin drying up, hungry fish may attack and kill humans.

From Iquitos, the sluggish, muddy Amazon curves like a snake, traveling the next 2,300 miles (3,710 kilometers) through warm, humid, mosquito-filled lowlands. In all of that long journey, the river descends only 300 feet (91 meters) in elevation. This part of the river and the surrounding forest is what is usually meant by the term Amazon or Amazonia. (People do not consider the high, cold mountain region at the start of the Amazon River as part of Amazonia.) If you are exploring these warm waters, pinkish gray Amazon river dolphins may frolic and follow your boat. Be sure to save plenty of time for your Amazon journey, because the river is 4,000 miles (6,450 kilometers) long, which makes it the second-longest river on earth!

THE COLORS OF A RIVER

If you travel the Amazon region, you'll notice that the river water varies in color. The Rio Tapajós has clear water. Near Manaus, Brazil, the muddy light-brown water of the Amazon River joins with the darker, tea-colored water of the Rio Negro. For more than 10 miles (16 kilometers) you can see the two colors of water flowing side by side, in the same channel, until they finally mix.

A river's color reflects what pours into it. The Rio Negro, for instance, is stained dark brown because rainfall passes through the leaves of the surrounding forest plants. These leaves, like tea leaves, contain lots of tannin, which stains the water brown. The Amazon, on the other hand, is muddy, and light brown because it carries so much clay. Rain washes this material off the surrounding land and carries it into the river. The color of river water is important because it indicates what chemicals are in the water. These chemicals, in turn, help determine what kinds of animals and plants can live in the river and on its banks.

ONE BIG RIVER, ONE BIG BORE

When you talk about the Amazon River, you have to talk in big terms. As much as 6 miles (9.7 kilometers) wide, the Amazon River carries more water than any other river on earth. It pours so much river water into the Atlantic Ocean that a sailor 62 miles (100 kilometers) out at sea can still see the muddy water coming from the river. If those figures do not impress you, just consider that in places the Amazon River is so wide you cannot see from one bank to another. And lying in the river mouth, is Marajó Island, which is bigger than Maryland, Delaware, and Rhode Island, combined!

At the Amazon's mouth, where it pours into the ocean, river water is affected by ocean tides, which push against it. When the high tide enters the river, it forms a wave called a tidal bore. Twice a year there is a *pororoca*, meaning a "big roar." A pororoca is a particularly large tidal bore, which can be 12 or more feet (as much as 4 meters) tall! Local people watch the slow, predictable wave pass by, staying out of its way.

FISH IN THE TREES

Where does the Amazon River end and the Amazon forest begin? At times it can be difficult to tell. During the rainy season, which begins in November, the lower Amazon River starts rising. Eventually it floods the surrounding forest. Fish actually swim among the branches of trees, eating fruit. You could canoe right through the treetops, and be eye to eye with monkeys, parrots, and macaws! This flooded forest, called the *várzea*, covers a little less than 2 percent of the Amazon region. The várzea, and other riverside areas have very rich soils, because the flooding Amazon deposits soil, decaying leaves, and other material, fertilizing the land.

Like squirrels in North American forests, fish in the várzea help plant trees in new places. Here's how it works: Fish eat fruit from a tree. Then the fish swim to other areas. Seeds from the fruit they ate pass through their bodies undigested, and are deposited in their droppings. The floodwaters recede. The seeds sprout, and presto! A new tree grows!

ON SOLID GROUND: TROPICAL RAIN FORESTS

In addition to várzea, Amazonia contains terra firma—dry land—forests that do not flood. This is where you will find the largest area of tropical rain forest on earth. Almost two thirds of this rain forest is in Brazil. But the rest extends into Bolivia, Colombia, Ecuador, French Guiana, Guyana, Peru, Suriname, and Venezuela.

Tropical rain forests may not flood, but they do get plenty of rain: 80 to 120 inches (203 to 305 centimeters) per year. Trees grow tall. Their leafy canopies, which are their umbrellalike tops, shade the forest floor below, blocking out 98 percent of the sunlight from above. So plant growth is not very dense on the forest floor. You can walk easily among the tree trunks, many of which are flared and folded, like swirled skirts. Massive folds, called buttresses, extend out to the sides of tree trunks and may help to keep tall trees from falling over.

Most mature tropical rain forests are not like the jungle you see in movies—a forest so thick with undergrowth that you need a machete to cut your way through. The jungle occurs mostly along roads and rivers. In these places the sunlight reaches the forest floor, so tropical vines, bushes, and other plants grow thickly and may block your path.

Tropical rain forests have many layers of life. The "roof" of the forest is the canopy layer, where leafy treetops gather sunlight. A few extremely tall trees, 25 to 75 feet (22 to 76 meters) tall, stick up above the canopy, here and there. These trees, called emergents, are home to sloths, long-armed, slow-moving mammals that dine on tree leaves. Algae grow on the sloth's moist fur, making it look slightly green.

Below, in the canopy, tree branches are draped with vines and loaded with epiphytes such as bromeliads. Bromeliads, which are members of the pineapple family, have overlapping leaves that form vases that fill with rain. Inside these rain pools, which may contain as much as 30 gallons (114 liters) of water, insect larvae hatch, frogs lay eggs, tadpoles grow up, and crabs live their entire lives. It's like a mini-pond on a tree branch, way up in the air!

Bromeliads, growing throughout the rain forest canopy, provide pondlike habitats in the treetops!

The canopy is the most active part of the forest. Toucans, which are colorful, big-beaked birds, crack open nuts and fruit. Howler monkeys howl while spider monkeys run along branches, using their tails like extra hands to grasp branches. The next layer down is the understory, where palm trees grow and vines climb tree trunks. But keep your eyes peeled, what looks like a vine might be a tree boa, wrapped around a branch instead! In the understory, blue morpho butterflies slowly flutter through the forest and down to the next layer, the forest floor. On the forest floor, ocelots—a kind of wild cat—roam and poison arrow frogs hop. (By the way, poison arrow frogs got their name because their skin contains a deadly poison once used on the arrow tips of native Amazonian hunters!) On tree trunks, and on the forest floor, large-leaved plants gather dim light that filters from above. You might recognize some of these plants. Many, such as philodendrons, are raised and sold as houseplants because they do well in the dim light of offices and homes.

IT'S IN THE TREES

One thing you won't see on the rain forest floor is a thick layer of leaves. Leaves decay and are recycled quickly in the warm, humid rain forest. (Plus, the leaves do not drop almost all at once, as they do in autumn in the temperate deciduous forests of the eastern United States.) Dead leaves and dead animals may get caught on tree branches or vines, and go through the process of decay there, never reaching the forest floor. This recycling of nutrients keeps the rain forest green and lush. But the soil below receives few nutrients, and is usually thin and infertile. That is why, when rain forest trees are cut and removed, nutrients are taken away from the forest, and very little grows back. This also explains why growing crops on cleared rain forest land requires continual applications of fertilizer.

HOPE YOU LIKE ANTS!

If you are walking in the Amazon rain forest and hear a strange rustling, an odd buzzing, and bird whistles, you may have found an army ant swarm. At night thousands of army ants join legs and bodies to form a ball called a bivouac. At dawn this living ball of ants breaks apart and the ants spread out across the forest floor. The ants catch and eat insects, lizards, frogs, and other small animals in their path.

Following the ant swarm are many species of antbirds. When insects fly up or run away to escape the ants, antbirds swoop in to catch them! (They do not eat the ants because ants' bodies contain formic acid, which is distasteful to most birds.) Parasitic flies follow the ants, too, laying eggs on the ants' backs. The eggs, when they hatch, produce larvae that eat the ants. Finally, butterflies fly behind the swarm, feeding on the antbirds' droppings. Army ants are not particularly dangerous to people, but you might want to wear tall boots and stand outside of the swarm, because ant bites do sting!

Army ants on the march eat mostly insects, which fly up to escape the swarm.

If you walk through the rain forest, do watch out for bullet ants. About 1 inch (2.5 centimeters) long, these ants have large pincers and a painful bite. But there's no need to worry about the columns of leaf-cutter ants that snake along forest paths. Leaf-cutter ants are fungi farmers. They cut and carry leaves to their nests, where they grow fungi on the leaves, then have a fungi feast!

Even if you don't see an army ant swarm or bullet ants or leaf-cutter ants, you are likely to see many other rain forest ants. E. O. Wilson, a famous biologist, once found 43 different species of ants on a single rain forest tree!

DAZZLING DIVERSITY

The Amazon rain forest has more than lots of different ants. It has many different species. An acre (or hectare) of tropical rain forest can have ten times as many tree species as you would find in the same size forest plot in Vermont. Birds, too, are more diverse in the tropical rain forest, and in the tropics. About 900 bird species have been seen in all of Canada and the United States. Yet more than half of that, as many as 500 bird species, can be seen in just a few square miles (or square kilometers) of the Amazon! In that same area, you might find 80 or more different kinds of frogs, and probably too many insect species to count. Biodiversity is higher in tropical rain forests than in any other place on earth.

THE AMAZON IN DANGER: DEFORESTATION

Each year more and more of the Amazon rain forest is being cleared. Some of the forest is cut by timber companies for rosewood, mahogany, and other tropical woods, which are used in furniture and other products. Some rain forest acreage is drowned when the course of rivers is changed in order to build dams, which produce electricity. Rain forest is also cut to clear land for raising cows. But day to day, much of the forest is being cleared tree by tree, by poor farmers trying to make a living off the land. (Over the years, the Brazilian government has also encouraged development of the Amazon by building roads through it, and by building a large capital city, Brasília, in the middle of the forest.)

In Brazil, most of the land that is good for farming and ranching is owned by only a very few people. So the rest of the Brazilian population must make a living as best they can. This is difficult because, like many parts of the world, the Brazilian population is increasing rapidly. Near cities people live in *favelas*, slums with leaky shacks made of scrap lumber, cloth, and metal tacked together, where there is usually no clean water and very little food.

Each time the government, a mining company, or a lumber company builds a road into the Amazon, people who do not own land follow the road, then spread out into the forest and make clearings. Hoping for a better life, these farmers move in, cut down the trees, and then burn the slash—the undergrowth left behind. Burning the slash clears the

PRODUCTS OF THE AMAZON

The Amazon has always been a rich source of natural products. Natural rubber comes from sap that drips out of rain forest trees. Chicle, the world's first chewing gum, was made from sap, too, but of a different rain forest tree. Brazil nuts and many delicious fruits come from the rain forest as well. And in the tropical forest of the eastern Andes grows the cinchona tree, the source of quinine, a drug that helps fight malaria, a sometimes deadly disease. So far, only a tiny fraction of rain forest plants have been studied for their medicinal benefits, or for their use in other products. If rain forests are destroyed, people will lose not only a wondrous habitat but also the potential for life-saving drugs and other valuable products.

Slash-and-burn agriculture, a necessity for poor farmers of the region, is destroying more and more of South America's rain forest.

land, and the ash from burning fertilizes the soil for the first few years. However, the nutrients in the soil are soon used up, and the farm becomes unproductive. Slash-and-burn agriculture, practiced in this way, is a tragedy for both the people and the rain forest. The rain forest cannot grow back, because too many of these areas, covering too much land, are being cut. Very small cleared areas in the midst of a rain forest can eventually heal. But larger areas cannot. Instead, heavy rains wash away the soil, which is no longer held by the tree roots. This clogs the rivers with silt. Meanwhile, to avoid going hungry, the farmers must move to another area and cut still more forest.

THE FOREST MAKES IT RAIN

Half of the Amazon's rainfall begins as moisture from the Atlantic Ocean. But the other half comes from the forest itself. Rain that falls on the forest travels through an endless cycle and is returned to the clouds. Here is how the cycle works: After a rainstorm, the heat of the sun evaporates moisture from wet leaves in the rain forest canopy. Some water from inside the trees is also given off through stomates, tiny openings in leaves, through a process called evapotranspiration. In a single day, 200 gallons (760 liters) of water may be released by a single tree. Hot air carries this water, as water vapor, up into the air, where it cools, condenses, forms clouds, and eventually rain.

When a large area of tropical rain forest is cut and cleared, the rain cycle is broken. From a plane you can see that many clouds hang over patches of forest, but few to none hang over the deforested land. Land stripped of forest bakes in the hot tropical sun and can become desertlike and infertile. Scientists are concerned that cutting large patches of the Amazon rain forest may someday make the Amazon a drier place overall.

PART OF THE PICTURE

Have you heard of greenhouse gases? They have scientists worldwide worried. Greenhouse gases act like the glass panes on a greenhouse, allowing sunlight into the earth's atmosphere, but not allowing all the sunlight-generated heat to escape. These gases perform a service, helping to keep the earth warm. But lately, the quantity of greenhouse gases has increased markedly, and this may be changing the earth's climate. Excess greenhouse gases are coming from vehicle exhaust, factory emissions, and the burning of forests, among other sources. Already the earth's overall air temperature is increasing. This warming could cause rising sea levels, animal and plant extinctions, and shifts in weather patterns.

The Amazon rain forest helps combat the greenhouse effect because it is one of the earth's biggest absorbers of carbon dioxide, a greenhouse gas. Each day, plants take in carbon dioxide from the air and use it in photosynthesis, the making of sugars that build the plants' leaves, roots, shoots, flowers, and fruits. As you might guess, all those

Amazon trees and plants, put together, remove a lot of carbon dioxide from the atmosphere. Cutting and burning the forest causes a double whammy—because it eliminates forest, which uses up carbon dioxide, and it also releases carbon dioxide through the process of burning.

The tropical rain forest, because it is such a huge mass of plants, affects many cycles on earth. It affects the rain cycle of the region and the carbon dioxide content of the

PEOPLE OF THE AMAZON

When the Spanish arrived in South America in the 1500s, an estimated 6 million native people, belonging to hundreds of distinctive tribes, lived in Amazonia. These native people had rich cultures and a vast knowledge of the forest, its animals, and its plants. Today, an estimated 150,000 native people remain in Amazonia; they speak 180 different languages. Their numbers have declined as outsiders have moved onto their lands. Some native people have been murdered outright. Others have died because of diseases accidentally introduced by Europeans. (Native Amazonians are often much more vulnerable to diseases that their people have never been exposed to.) Other

native people have been driven off their lands by miners, lumbermen, farmers, and governments with development plans.

Today the remaining people, such as the Yanomami, are trying to defend their way of life and their land. The Brazilian government has set aside some land for native Amazonians. The Yanomami have worked through the courts and the government to safeguard their land. But the battle continues, as gold miners and other settlers illegally move into the forests belonging to native peoples of the Amazon.

A Yanomami boy prepares to hunt, following the traditional ways of his people.

atmosphere. It absorbs and slows down heavy tropical rains. The more scientists understand about the Amazon rain forest, the more they appreciate the ways it stabilizes the climate, not only of South America but of the entire planet.

CONSERVATION EFFORTS IN SOUTH AMERICA

Conservation organizations and environmental efforts are not yet widespread in South America. But from the Amazon rain forest, to the highest Andean peaks, to the coral reefs of the Galapagos Islands, more and more people are working hard to conserve energy, protect forests, and save endangered animals and plants. Sometimes, protecting a natural area involves buying the land and setting it aside, as the Nature Conservancy and Ecotropica did when they bought 81,000 acres (32,780 hectares) of the Pantanal. But often, conservationists develop ways for local people to make a living off a natural area, without destroying it. This may involve returning to traditional methods of gathering medicines and foods, farming small plots within a forest, or hunting animals in carefully controlled hunting seasons. In other cases, ecotourism gives people an economic interest in protecting animals, plants, and habitats such as rain forests, wetlands, and grasslands.

Conservation is taking place in some South American cities, too. Jaimé Lerner, former mayor of Curitiba, Brazil, led his city of more than 1.6 million people to create a more environmentally friendly way of life. He spearheaded the creation of the city's efficient, high-speed bus system, which now carries more than two thirds of the people to and from work, cutting down on auto traffic and pollution. Under his guidance, the city began a tree-planting program and widespread recycling. About 50 to 70 percent of paper, plastic, and glass is recycled in Curitiba, among the highest recycling rates in the world! Favelas, the shack-filled slums that plague so many cities, are still a problem in Curitiba. But Lerner has helped clean up these areas and reduced health hazards by starting a garbage exchange program. People of the favelas can bring in their bags of garbage and exchange them for fresh vegetables or bus tickets. In this way, they help keep the streets clean, and receive nutritious food and much needed transportation. Free medical clinics and other programs help the poorest people of Curitiba, as well.

Environmental programs in the city of Curitiba, and elsewhere in South America, have become a source of environmental ideas for people around the world. Obviously, South America's natural wonders are not just its waterfalls, mountains peaks, and rain forests; but also its remarkable people.

GLOSSARY

altiplano—high plains in the Andes, near Lake Titicaca and La Paz, Bolivia

biodiversity—the variety of species of plants and animals in a given area

biome—an area that has a certain kind of climate and a certain kind of community of animals and plants

climate—a region's long-term weather conditions

cloud forest—rain forest that grows at middle to high elevations on mountainsides, and is often bathed in clouds and mist

deforestation—the destruction of forest by cutting, burning, or other means

desert—a biome that occurs where precipitation is less than 10 inches (25 centimeters) per year

ecotourism—the practice of traveling to natural areas to see their plants, animals, and natural beauty

El Niño—the shift in climate and ocean currents that occurs once every four to seven years in the Pacific

endemic—occurring in a specific area, and nowhere else

epiphyte—a plant that grows on other plants

glacier—a large, slow-moving mass of ice

greenhouse effect—warming of the earth caused by gases that act like the glass panes of a greenhouse, allowing sunlight into the earth's atmosphere, but only allowing some of the sunlight-generated heat to escape

greenhouse gases—gases in the atmosphere, including carbon dioxide and ozone, that cause the greenhouse effect

gran chaco—the swampy region drained by the Paraguay River, located in south central South America

llanos—grassy plains located in Venezuela and Colombia

pampas—grassy plains located in Argentina

Pangaea—the original landmass that existed 250 million years ago, when the separate continents we know today were all joined together

Pantanal—the world's largest wetland, made up of swamps and marshes in southwest Brazil

Panthalassa—the ocean that surrounded Pangaea

Patagonia—the region located at the southern tip of South America, mostly in Argentina

savanna—a type of grassland that has widely spaced trees

selvas—the forested region of the upper Amazon River

slash-and-burn agriculture—a type of farming in which people cut down the forest trees and burn the slash—the leftover crop debris—in order to clear the land for growing new crops

tectonic plate—a large piece of the earth's crust that slides over molten rock below, gradually shifting its position on the earth's surface

tropical rain forest—a forest biome found in the tropics and characterized by warmth, very heavy rainfall, and high species diversity

tropics—the region lying close to the equator, between the Tropic of Cancer and the Tropic of Capricorn

várzea—forest that is flooded by the Amazon River during the rainy season

wetland—land that is periodically flooded

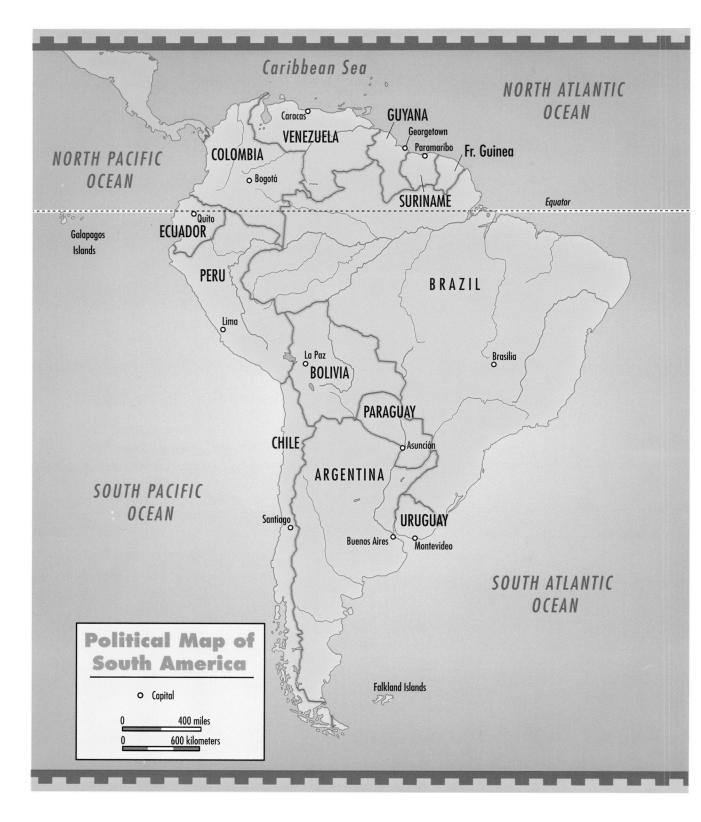

Caribbean Sea

NORTH ATLANTIC
OCEAN

NORTH PACIFIC
OCEAN

Caracas○

VENEZUELA

GUYANA

Georgetown○

COLOMBIA

Paramaribo○

Fr. Guinea

Bogotá○

SURINAME

Equator

Galapagos
Islands

Quito○

ECUADOR

PERU

BRAZIL

Lima○

La Paz○

Brasília○

BOLIVIA

PARAGUAY

CHILE

Asunción○

ARGENTINA

SOUTH PACIFIC
OCEAN

URUGUAY

Santiago○

Montevideo○

Buenos Aires○

SOUTH ATLANTIC
OCEAN

Falkland Islands

Political Map of South America

○ Capital

0   400 miles

0   600 kilometers

INDEPENDENT COUNTRIES LOCATED IN SOUTH AMERICA

NAME	CAPITAL
Argentina	Buenos Aires
Bolivia	La Paz
Brazil	Brasília
Chile	Santiago
Colombia	Bogotá
Ecuador	Quito
Guyana	Georgetown
Paraguay	Asunción
Peru	Lima
Suriname	Paramaribo
Uruguay	Montevideo
Venezuela	Caracas

DEPENDENCIES IN SOUTH AMERICA

Falkland Islands	British Crown Colony
French Guiana	Overseas department of France

FURTHER READING

BOOKS

(Books for young readers are marked with an asterisk.)

Arritt, Susan. *The Living Earth Book of Deserts*. Pleasantville, NY: Reader's Digest, 1993.

Bernard, Hans-Ulrich, producer. *Amazon Wildlife*. Boston: Houghton Mifflin, 1994.

* Blue, Rose, and Corinne Naden. *Andes Mountains*. Wonders of the World series. Austin, TX: Raintree Steck-Vaughn, 1995.

* *Central and South America*. Lands and People series, Vol. 6. Danbury, CT: Grolier, 1991.

Constant, Pierre. *The Galapagos Islands*. Lincolnwood, IL: Passport Books, 1995.

Dwyer, Christopher. *Chile*. Places and People of the World series. New York: Chelsea House, 1989.

Forsyth, Adrian, and Ken Miyata. *Tropical Nature: Life and Death in the Rain Forests of Central and South America*. New York: Scribner, 1984.

*Lourie, Peter. *Amazon: A Young Reader's Look at the Last Frontier*. Honesdale, PA: Caroline House, 1992.

*Pollard, Michael. *The Amazon*. Great Rivers series. New York: Marshall Cavendish, 1997.

Rice, Larry. *Baja to Patagonia: Latin American Adventures*. Golden, CO: Fulcrum Publishing, 1993.

*Sayre, April Pulley. *Tropical Rain Forest*. Exploring Earth's Biomes series. Brookfield, CT: Twenty-First Century Books, 1994.

Weiner, Jonathan. *The Beak of the Finch*. New York: Knopf, 1994.

SELECTED ARTICLES ABOUT SOUTH AMERICA

Chmielinski, Piotr, "Kayaking the Amazon: Through Wild Andes Rapids," *National Geographic*, April 1987, 461–473.

George, Uwe, "Venezuela's Islands in Time," *National Geographic*, May 1989, 525–561.

Graves, William, editor, "Amazonia: A World Resource at Risk," *National Geographic*, August 1992, map insert.

Margolis, Mac, "Treasuring the Pantanal," *International Wildlife*, November/December 1996, 12–21.

McIntyre, Loren, "The High Andes: South America's Islands in the Sky," *National Geographic*, April 1987, 422–459.

Van Dyk, Jere, "The Amazon," *National Geographic*, February 1995, 2–40.

Webster, Donovan, "The Orinoco: Into the Heart of Venezuela," *National Geographic*, April 1998, 8–31.

WORLD WIDE WEB

Web sites come and go very quickly, so it is best to use a search program to look for key words and phrases such as El Niño, Atacama, Amazon, and so on. Below are a few sites you may want to check:

USA Today's El Niño Information
Articles, maps, statistics, and links to other El Niño sites:

http://www.usatoday.com/weather/nino/wndoing.htm

NOAA (National Oceanic and Atmospheric Administration) El Niño site
Articles, maps, and statistics on El Niño worldwide:

http://www.ogp.noaa.gov/enso/news.htm/

INDEX

Page numbers in *boldface italics* refer to illustrations.